Contents

The library 4

Using the library 8

Librarians 12

Borrowing books 16

Learning 20

Glossary 22

Find out more 23

Comprehension questions 24

Index 24

The library

The library is a busy place to visit. Lots of people use the library every day.

A Visit to
The Library

Revised Edition

Blake A Hoena

Raintree is an imprint of Capstone Global Library Limited, a company incorporated in England and Wales having its registered office at 264 Banbury Road, Oxford, OX2 7DY – Registered company number: 6695582

www.raintree.co.uk
myorders@raintree.co.uk

Editorial credits
Sarah Bennett, designer; Tracy Cummins, media researcher, Laura Manthe, production specialist

Photo credits
Alamy: Randy Duchaine, 19; Capstone Press: Gary Sundermeyer, Cover, 7, 11, 15, 21; Getty Images: Blend Images, 17; iStockphoto: asiseeit, 5, kali9, 13; Shutterstock: amirage, Design Element, Rob Marmion, 9

Printed and bound in India

ISBN 978 1 4747 5633 4 (hardback)
22 21 20 19 18
10 9 8 7 6 5 4 3 2 1

ISBN 978 1 4747 5643 3 (paperback)
23 22 21 20 19
10 9 8 7 6 5 4 3 2 1

British Library Cataloguing in Publication Data
A full catalogue record for this book is available from the British Library.

The library is filled with shelves.

Each shelf holds many books.

Using the library

Library visitors do research.

They use computers and books

to look for information.

Visitors sit quietly.

Some read books for fun.

Other visitors study.

Librarians

The library has many books to read. Librarians help visitors find the right book.

Librarians read picture books

during story time.

Children and adults listen

to the story.

Borrowing books

Visitors can borrow books for
a few weeks. A librarian scans
the visitor's library card.

The library has lots of
other materials to borrow.
Visitors borrow DVDs,
magazines and audiobooks.

Learning

A library is a good place
to read and learn.

Sea

the Sea 1, 2, 3. Learn to count
ea stars, octopuses, and

y fun when you have colorful
orful foods, and other objects
nning readers can enjoy
eacher or parent.

Titles in this series:

Baby Animals 1,2,3
A Counting Book of Animal Offspring

Eating Pairs
Counting Fruits and Vegetables by Twos

Under the Sea 1,2,3
Counting Ocean Life

3,2,1 Go!
A Transportation Countdown

ISBN 0-7368-1477-1

90000>

9 780736 816779

Under the Sea
Counting Ocean Life

by Barbara Knox

Glossary

library card card with a person's name and library number printed on it; people use library cards to borrow materials from the library; they promise to bring back the materials on time and in good shape

materials items at a library that people can read or borrow; magazines, newspapers, videos, CDs, audiobooks and books are library materials

research look for; library visitors look for book titles or certain subjects on computers

scan use a machine that passes a beam of light over the code on a library card

story time time when children and adults gather to listen to a story read out loud

Find out more

Books

Librarian (People Who Help Us) Rebecca Hunter, (Tulip Books Ltd., 2017)

Librarian (Busy People) Lucy M George, (QED Publishing, 2017)

Websites

www.readingagency.org.uk/children
Find out about reading clubs, challenges and more at this website.

www.wordsforlife.org.uk
The National Literacy Trust's website offers some fun activities for children and advice for parents.

Comprehension questions

1. What does a librarian do at the library?

2. Name some of the materials you can find at a library.

3. Describe what you like best about the library.

Index

adults 14
borrow 16, 18
children 14
computers 8
DVDs 18
information 8
learn 20
librarians 12, 14, 16
library card 16
listen 14

magazines 18
materials 18
quietly 10
read 10, 12, 14, 20
research 8
scans 16
shelf 6
story time 14
study 10